Aquamarine

Aquamarine
Copyright © 2014 Yoko Danno
Paperback ISBN: 978-0-9840352-7-4

All rights reserved: except for the purpose of quoting brief passages for review, no part of this book may be reproduced or transmitted in any form or by any means, electronic or mechanical, including photocopying, recording, or by any information storage and retrieval system, without permission in writing from the publisher.

Cover art: "Hiraku – *Blossom of Hope*" by Pd Lietz
Interior art: Extract from "Hiraku – *Blossom of Hope*" by Pd Lietz
Cover design: Steven Asmussen
Design & Layout: Steven Asmussen

Glass Lyre Press, LLC.
P.O. Box 2693
Glenview, IL 60026

www.GlassLyrePress.com

Aquamarine

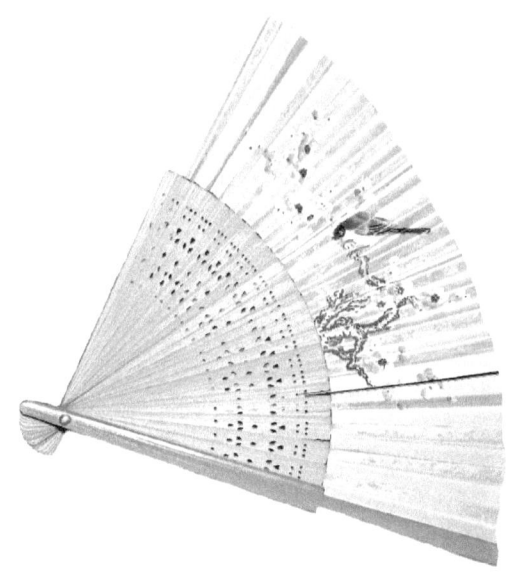

Yoko Danno

Acknowledgements

The author gratefully acknowledges to the editors and publishers of the following magazines, journals and anthologies, online or/and printed, where the poems first appeared, some of which were later changed slightly for this book:

poem, home: An Anthology of Ars Poetica: "behind the words"

Poetry Kanto: "stone steps echo," "river song," "road home, a mystery," "catfish in the woods"

Sunrise from Blue Thunder (*Pirene's Fountain*): "Blue Flower"

YOMIMONO 15, 17: "Beyond the Soot," "Festival Moon," "Flower Arrangement," "Door to Tap"

4W: "behind the door"

Otoliths 15, 21, 25, 29: "fool's gold," "aquamarine," "narrow pathway," "at random," "eater is eaten," "below the surface," "fall from a bell tower," "departure," "tell it to the stone"

ekleksographia #1: "on parting," "wild wind," "ubiquitous zero"

Praxilla #1, #2: "fire meets water," "birds before flight," "Morning Walk"

Pinstripe Fedra: "coffered ceiling"

Big Bridge: "all around is slow death," "into the shades," "vision, an owl, the eyes"

Dan Murano's Website : "necklace," "water city," "On the Trail of a Dog"

First Water: Best of Pirene's Fountain: "fire realm"

Beverage Anthology (*Pirene's Fountain*) : "beyond the tropics"

at night
a man
taps softly
on a
wooden
door.

                    a woman
                    slips
                    in and out
                    of her dreams
                    at will.

—James C. Hopkins, *eight pale women**

*The Word Works, Washington, D. C., 2003

Contents

I. Behind the Words
- behind the words   13
- moon appearing   14
- eardrums beat   15
- fool's gold   16
- stone steps echo   17
- beyond the tropic   18

II: Fire Meets Water
- fire meets water   22
- fire realm   23
- catfish in the woods   24
- water city   25
- necklace   26
- coffered ceiling   27

III: Before Flight
- birds before flight   30
- long before sunset   31
- fall from a bell tower   32
- departure   33
- aquamarine   34
- at random   35

IV: ON PARTING
- on parting   38
- wild wind   39
- all around, slow death   40
- eater is eaten   41
- into the shade   42
- ubiquitous zero   43

V: Sound is an Inspiration
- crack of dawn — 46
- behind the door — 47
- listening eyes — 48
- snake dancer — 49
- river song — 50
- tell it to the stone — 51

VI: Message in the Air
- message in the air — 54
- narrow pathway — 55
- vision, an owl, the eyes — 56
- below the surface — 57
- road home, a mystery — 58
- at sea — 59

Coda: Dream, Love & Death
- Blue Flower — 62
- Morning Walk — 64
- Door to Tap — 66
- Festival Moon — 68
- Beyond the Soot — 70
- On the Trail of a Dog — 72

I. BEHIND THE WORDS

1 behind the words

written at all hazard
despite riots, curfews and typhoons
is a language unheard of –

the language of fish
painted on the arched ceiling
of an ancient shrine
revived by a touch
of salt water,

spoken as well by trees and animals
in a blind younger world
before literate humans arrived,

when a leaf was heavier than gold
                        and silver dust still falling
                                        from the moon –

a story starts
    at the center behind a seer's eyes,

        child monks parrot the words
                                  diligently
        with tears in their eyes –

from the bottom
of a salt lake,
dry and long forgotten,

rises a faraway laughter
like a ripple of mirage over water.

2 moon appearing

a dream is just behind the door –
clap your hands twice
at the back of your head
                          and enter

under a spell of curves
tendrils, spirals, circles
hanging from a fir tree
luminous on silver strings,

wade through waves of light
to the place of your birth,
where white flower petals fall
without a breeze, sweeping

into a next dream – a pair
of white tigers appear
in a dewy gardenia bush
flirting with each other
                          daringly,

sweat around their necks
turning into prayer beads
scatters among fireflies –

it was over
before i knew when
a door was just behind the dream.

3 eardrums beat

a man
      and
            a woman
fragile
     like
           distant
     music
across
     a dark
         river
              shout
        seed
     syllables
at the top
     of their
         silent
             voices
                  in the land
                        of fertile
                 dragons

until fish begin to swim
     until vocal muscles give out –

          eardrums beat
         offbeat
          throbs
           slip
             down
               the
                  throats

               eyes blink inward.

4 fool's gold

    now   up
              now   down
      like   color
          socks   in
            a
                      drier
            my
    thoughts
               whirls

even before a major typhoon arrives –

    absent-minded
        or without mind
    in crossing swords
        with a praying
                      mantis
    most importantly
        breathe at ease
                        free
      from the ringing
               in your memory –

if you are hungry
    after a warm-up
        have some chocolate

    wrapped in silver foil
        with a slip of paper
                  with words:

    "mica flakes, fool's gold"

5 stone steps echo

in the moonlit woods
    birds huddle in their nests,
the footsteps receding,
    a woman hides herself
inside a shrine from
    gossiping neighbors –

through the open window
    a wind blows
        grasshoppers hum
            off her mind,

    dimly lit, bats
        chatter with radar
    from brain to brain
        in search of a vent
    in an invisible dome
        eyes closed tight
            as rosebuds,

dew-lit leaves leading her dance,
    soaked in timid light
her steps draw an open circle,
    pigeons fed with frozen
              rime –

she rests like a stick of celery
    in tomato juice – a monkey-god
            is born
when the wind blows her cover
    finally from the sea of her womb.

6 beyond the tropic

when the die is cast,
    whether or not to cross the line,
        oh, the difference!

there's nothing to fear
under the tropical water
where shadows disappear
and dreams come to life.

rolling through inviting
kelp, a woman wakes
to an undersea castle
at the foot of a rainbow

to meet the real her again
where colors and forms
of yesterdays are blurred
where even she disperses.

pink pelicans fade amiss
into layers of deep blue
where invisible stars
dead eons ago shine cold.

flying fish disturb her vigil
as they leap into thin air,
the scales reflecting light
glance like multiple eyes.

she toasts with ambrosia
after crossing the tropics
when crabs return ashore
half drunk with fresh water.

II: FIRE MEETS WATER

1 fire meets water

a steep descent is inevitable
                from a knife-edge,
     caught by a hail storm
              as sudden as an airburst –

the sky is below my eyes,
              the planet spinning
    as i fall
         through a deep open crack,
                      snow-blinded,
      a whistle of silence
                in my ear –

the fact is
    i'm not falling but ascending
        like hissing vapor
            when fire meets water

    as i plunge right into the basin
                of a waterfall
           with flaming torches

    into the body of an aqua god
          waiting for my arrival
                  not as a surprise

but with open arms
    spreading like white wings
                              ready to fly
        across the world's highest roof.

2 fire realm

mountains are ablaze,
        a fire god awakened
                by a slash of lightning
                        at the rock.

memories of minerals revived
        when the earth shakes
                revealing red chasms
                        like slit eyes.

a woman stumbles to her knees
        as she senses the tremor,
                her teeth chattering
                        with cold.

a shudder slides along
        the nape of her neck
                when she feels remote heat
                        beneath her feet.

at the back of her eyes
        lives a salamander –
                when will it be consumed
                        by its own fire?

3 catfish in the woods

my dog suddenly runs off
slipping the leash
startled by a wild beast –

without blowing
a conch, the giant
fish-god tosses and turns

in the deep ocean bed
heaving his bloated belly
in his millenary sleep –

the mischievous catfish*
plays dirty tricks
belching out muddy billows

over homes, rice paddies
boats, cars, nuclear plants
guzzling them all alive –

under a tree radioactive
rays filtering through
branches fall on my face.

*In Japanese folklore a giant catfish living underground causes earthquakes.

4 water city

reluctant to leave, but
estranged from urban life
by fancy-clad pedestrians
chattering in loud whispers,

a winged lion crouches
with the sun at its back
on leaping into upper gases
to finally leave the pedestal.

under a stone bridge
cormorants are hungry
after eating their fill
ready to swallow more.

what's happening below
the glittering surface
of the canal water? dust
falling from smiling angels.

for a visitor demanding
an immediate answer
a tangible clue available
is a roach-ridden room.

with chocolate and wine
shift only for yourself
in this sunset-flooded city
till shadows lead the way.

5 necklace

talking leaves
written on the parchment

parchment, dry and curled   behind the kitchen table
in the heat wave   a beast of a shadow looms up
winter isn't far behind   begging for flower petals

flower petals scattered   sea dragons, sea lions
on a shrine's white gravel   anemones among sea weeds
sun above the fog of sea   together in our party tonight

tonight, moonless and starless   a knife cut into a roast pig
concealed behind rocks   in the fuming room
assassin sharpens his knife   pass me the salt, please

please pepper the dull   burners burning the jungle
sentence – fragrance   alive – no nests, no calling
rises from incense burners   of the wild – the coast is clear

clear morning, doves mourn
on MaDonNa's lap

6 coffered ceiling

a yellow lotus   on a severed head
a black lotus   in a mouth agape
a green lotus   in a hand with eyes
a white lotus   in a coiled snake

between dim light
& amber shadow
before a spray of
orange is offered

a seed is what   i hide in my pocket
space is where   to share it with you
home is when   you live with a peach
& a white skull   washed up on a beach

III: BEFORE FLIGHT

1 birds before flight

in the pale morning mist
    a swan
        ruffles her feathers,
                hunting for
            breakfast
        plunges her head,
                eyes
        wide open,
            into the sun
                in the water.

yesterday's laughter
    at a picnic
        still lingers
            like geese before
                migrating north
        at the edge of a pond.

lacking
    in herd instinct
        an owl is ever-alert,
            eyes half-shut
                in the light
                as in meditation,
            perched between the fishtails
                      on a temple roof,

    pondering why
            he is up there
                  before knowing
              how to tell time
                      in the woods.

2 long before sunset

just like
    a squirrel leaves his drey
                in the oak tree
     without calculating
        the loss and gain
                of acorns
    not because the sky
        is threatening
   nor he is alarmed
      by a desperate easel's
              final fart,

before afternoon tea
   before wine
       invested
               in vain
   before
     his brain
        clouded

   because the nesting hole trims
              the landscape
        beyond his vision,

he sets out
        for a new horizon

   before the fire
     in the hearth
        gives off sparks,

   before the sun sets gloriously
               as never seen before.

3 fall from a bell tower

    sirens blare out
   an ambulance
     with hopes
       &
    oxygen
    bombs
    rushing
   to the
   scene
    of
   her fall,

keep staring
     in   her   fugitive
       eyes
           stirring
          like   dust
     over   an
          arid   pathway

if they don't see
            you
      as if tightly locked
                from inside,

don't cry your heart out
but keep looking into her eyes
until the windows
                  open

       and the engine
              starts.

4 departure

as if urged
by scurrying fallen leaves
birds of passage
fly into thin air

a pair of
fancy sandals
cast off
at the foot
of a staircase

keenly calling
cranes
fade
beyond
snowy peaks

the sky
is a bridge
between there
and here

the depth
only fathomed
through bare branches

5 aquamarine

hush!   a sign of
        a landslide!

  birds stop
        singing – no time
     to eat
         blueberries
            we have plucked
or re-lace
        our muddy
              boots!

        deep
        down
        rock
        walls
        melt
  through friction
     the live
   hot water
  crystallized
  into a tint
 of seawater
  in a bed
   of mica

the blue-green
  radiance
  confined
under my pillow

6 at random

volumes
       of
             vibrant
    life
      seeds
               dancing
    arranged
         without
                  will –

it happens
    in the right
    moment
    in the right
    space
    between right
    elements

in magma
    four million years
                   old

or in the soft
       tissues
          of
       human brains
               in love –

         a crystalline union

IV: ON PARTING

1 on parting

    buy
    good
    mud
    for flowers
    don't
    get mad
    at a
    cactus
    on part-
              ing

            a party
            goes
            on as
             long
        as muddlers
        bend
        in   cock-
        tail
        glasses

    sing
    a spider
    's
    ding-
    dong
    song
    to solace
              your prize

2 wild wind

after
midnight
when
a tiger
meets
a rabbit
what
will he
       eat?

monks
in
black
meditate
                bats
                hang
                upside
                down
                sounding
                alarm

when
   you
      sense
         a wall
            in the
               dark
                  lean
                     on a
                        wild
                           wind

3 all around, slow death

a flash
    of fireworks
        is preferred
            to life
          support

    blood
      vessels
        twist
          & turn
      sound-
      less-ly
      as in deep
        intoxication

    bubbles
rise
    spar-
      kling
        in red
          & green
        fruit drinks

  a balloon
    explodes
          at the tip
      of my
        naked
     finger

4 eater is eaten

if grains
of sand
get
into your
shoes

       don't
       look back
       your unborn
       will get
       injured

a beast
of a shadow
follows
you
a trail

       of hoof-
       prints
       from
       the brink
       of a swamp

he is
at your
heels
eating your
dreams

       whenever
       you are not
       on your toes
       the eater
       is eaten

   when the mud settles

5 into the shade

like rescue
ropes
wisteria
flowers
hanging
from
the trellis

pigeons &
  passersby
      swirling
         around
           huge
          yellow
        umbrellas
    in eddies
in galaxies

a flock
of black
birds
flying wild
to the womb
of pink
    gold
        ruby hours

dark
glasses
are essential
to gaze
into ultra
      violent rays

6 ubiquitous zero

    a bird's-eye view
        of a medieval city
            before going to bed
      with a
      glass
      of wine

      all
      roads
      closed
      in the
      valley
          below

separate greens
    from plastic
        for disposal
    ubiquitous
    zero
    unites
    with
    every
    oxygen

a miraculous birth
      of a goldfish
          at the ocean's
  depths
  out of
  its old skin
      into
          dark-consuming
              light

V: SOUND IS AN INSPIRATION

1 crack of dawn

roosters crow at 4 a.m.
in a fishing village
before a ferryboat leaves port —

quivering in the cool air
a lunar moth spreads its wings
after casting off its skin.

no time to rest quietly
in the hissing sound of light
filtering through tea leaves,

broken free from darkness
by the departure gong
into blank space within noise,

it flutters shyly and shines
on the invisible strings
vibrated by a million moths

sipping at concealed honey,
energy through its body flowing
into the eyes on its wings,

wide open on the watch
for assaults from above.
waiting for the gossamer

cloud to disperse, it burns
for dear life, emitting
signals to thirsty females.

2 behind the door

where are you from?

tat-tat-tat on the door,
the sun is already up –
start weeding the garden
before mosquitoes' breakfast.

after a good sweeping
you can see with the eye
in your palm – hold it up
to the morning light.

place the warmed hand
over a wound pulsing
in the real skin under
the protective outer layer.

let the atoms dance
molecules twirl wildly
cells sing hallelujah
in c major in unison.

dance, dance, dance
with a whirlwind blowing
through your body, burn
dry leaves and trash!

in a bowl of green tea
is a world of the dead,
one-millionth of a micro-
millimeter behind the seen.

3 listening eyes

between
a pregnant
cloud
and
the ground
passes
a flashing
current

caught
in
a clap
of
thunder
i lost
my hearing

as if
trans-
muted
by a
lucent
black sound

in a
city
of silence
dew
on a honey-
suckle

tinkles
like wind-bells.

4 snake dancer

she dives again
s
w
o
o
p
!

the
smell
of
freshly
grated *wasabi*

the dance
and
the dancer
break
open
the egg

heads
together
tread
barefoot
on hot
embers

headfirst
into
an ocean

for emancipation
                underwater

5 river song

sing it to the frogs
        croaking in the paddy —

like a piece of soft wet silk
she presses her belly
onto a boulder in the river
feeling the dull throb

    of molten core
       erupted
    cooled, fissured
       saturated
    with moisture alive—

freed from
rice planting,
she swims underwater

to a man standing alone
under a cascade
immersed in the sound
of water rushing over rocks.

wakened from a summer
night's ecstatic dream,
the cobbles shimmer
on the riverbed —

    in the sunlight
       before spawning
           salmon are frantic.

6 tell it to the stone

beyond the leafless desert
an overblown reptile
reduced to white bones
in a timely sand storm,

tightly folded cactus roots
scorched almost to death
unfold from long sleep
with friendly showers.

a lotus unfurling
reveals a yellow eye
a secret, a manuscript
a wisp of memory.

tell it to the stone
in the swift early hours
between red and white
timeless time in space.

careful not to speak
underwater – unfathomable
mysteries long buried
will resurrect and survive.

VI: MESSAGE IN THE AIR

1 message in the air

after fasting in the forest
    in the precincts of a shrine
        a man is blowing
                a conch horn

no matter what
    the surrounding mountains
            echo the sound
    until it opens up
        the frozen sky —

a bright red ball sinking
below the horizon
at the meeting time
of the sky with the water,

a sutra
    open on my desk
        by candlelight

at a fish
    popping up
        above the text

                i blink —

a message
    in the air
        again back
            to water...

2 narrow pathway

if i turn
a somersault,
       gravity-free,
my
chance
to right myself
may slip through
fingers.

i have to decide
which end
is top
or bottom
as i tumble
in midair
in a nightmare
maze.

after seeing a child
glide down
the slide
in high glee
into purple dusk
i turn
over again
on a balance beam.

a fair landing – i am
prepared
for the birth

of my own mother.

3 vision, an owl, the eyes

far up north a sudden fall
    of temperature turns the mist
into hoarfrost, bare trees
    into white blossoms —

out of words into woods
    out of woods into words
i stroll among meanings

through layers of night
    out of words into a wind
from midair back to woods

seeking a thin word
    beneath another
hidden under a tough snow.

light diffused in whiteout
    contours of fir trees
fading into blurry skies,

icy leaves scintillating
    a deer burns its tongue
licking at the frozen bark.

untimely thunder rolling
    lightning reveals
an owl on the usual alert–

the penetrating eyes gleam
    between bare branches
just before i lose my senses.

4 below the surface

where are you going?

a ripple of sparkling
    light flattens
when it ceases to blow.

chitchat of the sun
    on the surface of water
quieting down to a lull,

without noticing
    the subtle moment
the wind falls to null.

we are born alone
    out of the shadows
and reborn into a blur,

as i float half-dead
    in the salt water
arise in deep silence

exquisite bodies, trans-
    lucent, still alive
wavering among weeds.

5 road home, a mystery

this side up! glass is in the box !
  a long journey is destined —

when we look up
while rotating
fixed in a Ferris wheel
an expanse of empty blue —

he likes diving for pearls,
    she prefers spacewalking,
he loves the tropical sea,
    she yearns for snow peaks,

    the same old story
        back and forth
    from white leopards
        to flamingo pink
    between song and sutra
        woven together

    by the weaver's will —

two minds
        in an ocean
    of seeds
        soon to be merged
                    into a whole
                churning
            evolving
                    without cease…

6 at sea

looking for a milestone
i follow in haste
a wavy line
along the water's edge
before it vanishes
washed by a new wave...

   with a scent of
                        seasonal wind
            waves break
                              into white foam
 ever-changing
              in unsettled
                          daylight
                          in response to the tide...

        after   a storm
              wings   scattered
                      antennae   bent
           white
                   butterflies
     without   markings...

i wade through water,
    weeds clinging to my ankles,
    shell's edge cutting my feet,

blindly
    heading home
        where i lived
            before my birth...

CODA: DREAM, LOVE & DEATH

1 Blue Flower

Moonlight illuminating my way, I hurried home in strange elation. Not that anything special had happened, but I saw the curb stone gleaming in the dusk. I had been to my dentist for the biannual medical check. Nothing was wrong with my teeth or gums. On my way back a phrase occurred to me over and again: The vacant lake is covered with fallen flower petals.

The cherry blossom season was over long before. As I walked on, suddenly a gust of wind blew from behind, and I looked back. A bright, white, full moon was in the eastern sky. Yellow dead leaves were blown up from the pavement ahead.

> In a woman's heart
>   a warm circulation of air.

I lit a candle and burned incense. I sat alone in my room, looking at a blue flower in print, shouldering years of silence. The flame wavered but the flower petals did not. I closed my eyes and the afterimage of the flower remained. When I opened my eyes the paper flower was gone, but I tried to keep seeing the blue flower.

I try to see the flower whenever I am awake, whenever I am alone, or even in a crowd. I try to describe the flower at every chance. It has become my second nature to try getting at it—with a birds-eye view from the balcony of a temple, by a feel of shadow under a weeping willow, by a smell at dead leaves in the damp ground, in the sky flashed by earthquake lightning. The moment I come to touch the tip of a petal, the flower will fade out. Feeling deluded, I usually retreat to my own flower garden.

> Delicate and feathery
>   high up in the blue sky
>   an island of fine white tendrils.

Comfortably fatigued from weeding the garden, I went to bed early. In my sleep I felt a strong wind blowing through my body and going out of the crown of my head. I almost fell backward when a monk supported me from behind. I didn't know he had been there. I had no idea who he was.

This morning I found a postcard in the mailbox. My long-awaited friend is coming back next spring. He has been away from home for a long time in search of the blue flower blooming only in the high Himalayas.

    As if waking from a deep sleep
        the purple sky turns
            into full blossom of stars.

2 Morning Walk

While strolling on a river bank I saw a pair of red camellias drifting down the river. Before I was aware I quickened my pace in an effort to catch up with the flowers. I remembered a couple of days before I had seen a camellia tree in full blossom on the upper reaches, the leaves shining in the afternoon sun as if made of green jade. I had broken off a spray with an unfolding flower bud so that I could arrange it with other tiny flowers in a bamboo basket—an offering to the spirit of harmony and quietude.

> *Incense is burning on the charcoal fire, water boiling in the iron kettle. The sand walls waver, reflecting the candlelight. The tea master tells me: "Perform the ceremony as if you were in a dream, but mind you, let your brains respond vividly to the sound and smell and light in the room, as in meditation."*

The memory of the green tea blew my mind and suddenly I wanted to smell the sea. I resumed walking and came to the mouth of the river. I took off my shoes as in entering a tea house. While making for the shoreline I felt my bare feet warm on the sand. There was no wind, but the glistening surface of the sea was rippled as if rocked incessantly by an invisible hand.

> *As I move the bamboo whisk rapidly in the bowl to make tea, plovers twitter on the beach. A breeze blows gently through the pine grove, the aroma of sandalwood in the air—an offering to the spirit of the sparkling haven.*

The shoreline began to retreat on the ebb. The pair of red camellia had disappeared into the thin mist. I hurried back home to make preparations for my guest from abroad. A shadow crossed the corner of my eye. I saw ahead a white heron alight in the shallows. I halted and watched the bird feeding itself. I gazed at it intently, as it looked up and saw me with one eye. I wished it would come to me, but at my slightest beckoning it flew away as if to respond to a call. I noticed its mate far up the river, also looking for fish.

3 Door to Tap

The door of the cuckoo clock opened, the bird came out, calling seven times. It was fine but windy as usual in early February. I looked up at the sky from the window of my room. A bright crescent was hiding behind the island of clouds—time to search for my star in the constellation of Orion, the dark blue Hunter.

All day I spent time trying to dig out a lost article. I couldn't remember what was missing while I was hunting for it. I rummaged through a lot of drawers before I found a box with picture postcards. It was the thing I had forgotten for a long time. A birthday present from my printer friend who had visited a village of Mali tribe in Africa. On each card is printed by hand a flower, or a star, or a tree, with a caption.

"The secret of life is to find your own star," one card tells. The seeds of life came to this planet from a far-off star, the Mali people believe. The home where your twin brother or sister lives. The letter attached to the box says, "My dear, you must find your guardian star that follows you throughout your lifetime."

On a sunny afternoon I wandered from room to room among sculptures in a museum, trying to find a door to a courtyard. Then I came to a bronze piece named "Gate of Return." It had no door but I dared enter through the opening of the sculpture. Not knowing if I was inside the Gate or outside, I looked around—shafts of sunlight falling like a shower of meteors.

The key to your dream, I've heard say, is to tap a door and open it—fountains dancing like flames, flower buds unfolding in the sun. The key lies in a tree that tells you where to find your star—between the twigs. Leaves will scatter from the tree like words from a mouth, whirling in the wind, while the trunk remains.

In the yard next door a woman is feeding a fire with bundles of letters. At times ashes flare up, smoke curling into the purple dusk. The smell of burning paper seeps into my room—a dog is barking—the setting sun casts a shadow like a horse-head nebula on the whitewashed wall. Orion's three stars are approaching the zenith.

4 Festival Moon

We had secretly arranged to meet at a crossroads on the eve of the Fire Festival held every year in June. The main road to the shrine was already filled with villagers in summer kimono, each with a round paper fan in hand. Night was falling softly like a monk's silk gauze robe. I was waiting for my twin brother to return across the mountain. I imagined him hurrying past by the pair of stone guardian deities at the entrance to our village. The full moon was behind a thin cloud, faintly illuminating the mountain ridge. He never appeared.

In my dream I had been struggling to remember a poem when I woke to the sound of shrill voices. The familiar scene of my favorite park was before my eyes—children playing tag. I was sitting on a bench, my feet steeped in the cool air. It dawned on me that what I had been groping for in the dream was a poem by a woman poet in 8th century, Japan. I had been the poet, waiting for her brother and lover who had been expelled from the village to a remote island, because he had revealed his illicit love in a poem:

> As if laying a hidden
> Irrigation pipe
> To a rice paddy
> On the mountainside
> Stealthily I courted
> My beloved sister!
> Secretly I wept
> Yearning after my loved one!*

She was determined to go her own way:

> It has been long since you set out.
> I will come to meet you
> Because I cannot wait any longer!*

The unfortunate lovers were forced to commit double suicide on each other's sword on the mountain across which they had tried to elope. A wind rustled the leaves of camphor trees. Crows cawed restlessly. I felt chilly and left the bench. I went up to the pond in the park and looked in the water. From the bottom a pair of huge carp, black and red, drawn to my reflection in the water, rose up and opened their mouths as if appealing to an audience.

The festival music, flutes and drums, grew faint, and abruptly a siren blared. An ambulance rushed past by the park. I thought it was just a usual pileup at the crossroads. When I learned that the driver and a woman in the passenger seat had been killed instantly, somehow it struck me as an accident that had happened far back in another century. The crows had ceased to caw. It was past time to take my children home but I kept watching them slide, one after the other, boldly into the purple and blue dusk. The moon revealed itself from behind the cloud, shining coldly like a polished bronze mirror.

The poems are quoted from the "Kojiki," a collection of Japanese songs and stories compiled in the 8th century (translated by Yoko Danno). The tragic story of the lovers is also based on a story in the book.

5 Beyond the Soot

Who put me here in this room,
   with the four blank walls, without a window?
A voice said, "You have three meals a day, don't worry."
What am I supposed to do? Paint the walls? Draw pictures?

I visited an old temple to see the mural paintings. The monk guiding us sightseers said, "Beneath the soot are dancing angels and celestial flowers in bloom," pointing to the blackened ceiling of the Paradise Hall that houses three images of Buddha. In this Hall, he mentioned, monk after monk has practiced for hundreds of years, burning candles and incense with the windows and doors shut, chanting sutras and meditating in effort to attain the Buddha's Pure Land.

After visiting the Paradise Hall I stood under a tall pine tree, absurdly expecting an apple to fall and hit my head. I tried to imagine the mind of the Lord Buddha or Mr. Newton, but I was distracted by a sudden wind. It scattered the fallen leaves that had been swept together from all over the temple garden. The green carpet of moss was patterned with maple leaves in all tints of red and yellow. Dogs were barking, in unison with a siren from my past.

I was in the ambulance with my father who'd had a stroke. He lay unconscious but when I placed my hand on his forehead he feebly tried to brush it off. I clasped his hand and it slightly responded. I knew where we were heading, but my eyes kept staring beyond our destination.

   His life feels like the eye
      of a huge transparent tornado.

To decorate the white hospital room I went home to pluck a rose in my garden. It was wet from rain and slipped through my hand. In panic I grabbed at it, and a thorn stuck deep into my forefinger. The pain traveled in waves like sound through water. As the pain abated I felt relaxed as if a coiled snake were unwinding in my body. When I returned to the hospital my father was still in a coma in the oxygen tent. Time seemed to have slipped from his grasp.

A breeze stirred the fringes of my hair. My thought flashed back to the Paradise Hall. I was sitting at the center of the whirling voices of monks chanting. The smoke from the burning candles and incense, mingled with the craving for ultimate peace of mind, curled up to the ceiling, covering the tangible heaven with soot. I breathed deeply several times. Rust came off my mind. I felt as if my body were gradually lifting into the smoky air, floating down the luminous river among rocks and blossoming apple trees.

6 On the Trail of a Dog

For four days my dog wouldn't eat or drink. I kept him inside the house, gave him water, milk, and even minced meat, but he refused to eat or drink. He wouldn't let me touch him, bristling at me. He was persistently within his own world, keeping me watchful of him day and night. On the fifth day he tottered to his feet and I let him go out. He urinated at his favorite fig tree in the corner of the backyard and came back, staggering. I decided to take him to a vet.

When I tried to take him down from my car, I found him unexpectedly soft and loose. The warm and spineless lump, heavy in my arms, lacked his usual stubbornness. He wasn't breathing, eyes wide open, without seeing me. He was gone. I wrapped him in a purple blanket and buried him under the fig tree with a lot of yellow and red roses.

Later at twilight I followed a dog, wading through a river, until I was on the verge of drowning. I climbed out of the water, then took a long trail through the darkening mountain, and finally into a familiar-looking house. When it grew light I was aware that the dog had turned into my beloved late uncle—presiding over the table of my late parents, cousins, aunts and uncles, celebrating my dead son's birthday.

On hurrying home from my family's grave:

>cherry blossoms
>>flare in a breath
>>>to be one

>>with a death
>>>in water —

Last night the temperature dropped sharply from 15°C to freezing zero. A chill was cast over the unfolding rose buds, due to bloom perpetually in bright yellow and deep red. To honor my dog's memory I definitely need the color purple in my flower garden. The problem is which to choose— sweet-smelling violets, or dark-centered asters, or a wistful wisteria twining its way from tree to tree.

About the Author

Photo: Doris G. Bagen

Yoko Danno is Japanese, living in Kobe. She writes poetry solely in English. Many of her poems have appeared internationally in anthologies, magazines and e-journals. She is the author of several poetry books and chapbooks, including *Epitaph for memories* (The Bunny and The Crocodile Press, USA, 2002), *The Blue Door*, a collaboration with James C. Hopkins (The Word Works, USA, 2006), and *Trilogy & Hagoromo: A Celestial Robe* (The Ikuta Press, Japan, 2010). *a sleeping tiger dreams of manhattan: poetry, photographs and sound,* by Danno, Hopkins and Bernard Stoltz (The Ikuta Press, 2008), was translated into Latvian and published by Mansards Publishing House (Riga, 2012). Her translation of Japanese myth and verse, *Songs and Stories of the Kojiki*, compiled in the 8th century, was published by Ahadada Books (Toronto/Tokyo, 2008).

Visit her website at **http://www.ikutapress.com/danno3.html/**

GLASS LYRE PRESS, LLC

"Exceptional works to replenish the spirit"

Poetry collections
Poetry chapbooks
Select short & flash fiction
Occasional anthologies

Glass Lyre Press is a small independent literary press interested in work which is technically accomplished and distinctive in style, as well as fresh in its approach and treatment. Glass Lyre seeks writers of diverse backgrounds who display mastery over the many areas of contemporary literature, writers with a powerful and dynamic aesthetic, and ability to stir the imagination and engage the emotions and intellect of a wide audience of readers.

The Glass Lyre vision is to connect the world through language and art. We hope to expand the scope of poetry and short fiction for the general reader through exceptionally well-written books which call forth our deepest emotions and thoughts, delight our senses, challenge our minds, and provide clarity, resonance and insight.

www.GlassLyrePress.com

www.ingramcontent.com/pod-product-compliance
Lightning Source LLC
Chambersburg PA
CBHW020627300426
44112CB00010B/1225